Journal Your Dreams Until They Take Wings

Tracking Your Goals and Dreams
Journal Your Journey

How Do I Get There?

Outer Direction and Inner Direction

Journal Your Dreams Until They Take Wings
JOURNAL YOUR JOURNEY

Julie Copeland Turner

WESTBOW
PRESS®
A DIVISION OF THOMAS NELSON
& ZONDERVAN

WestBow Press books may be ordered through booksellers or by contacting:

WestBow Press
A Division of Thomas Nelson & Zondervan
1663 Liberty Drive
Bloomington, IN 47403
www.westbowpress.com
1 (866) 928-1240

Scripture taken from the King James Version of the Bible.

Scripture taken from the Holy Bible, NEW INTERNATIONAL VERSION®. Copyright © 1973, 1978, 1984, 2011 by Biblica, Inc. All rights reserved worldwide. Used by permission. NEW INTERNATIONAL VERSION® and NIV® are registered trademarks of Biblica, Inc. Use of either trademark for the offering of goods or services requires the prior written consent of Biblica US, Inc.

ISBN: 978-1-5127-6229-7 (sc)

Library of Congress Control Number: 2016918084

Print information available on the last page.

WestBow Press rev. date: 11/30/2016

CONTENTS

1. Record Your Dreams 1

2. First Things First! 5

3. What Is Holding You Back? 6

4. Before a New Year, Remove Some Obstacles. 8

5. Let's Take a Good Look Inside 11

6. Goal Setting 13

7. New Motivation or Inspiration 15

8. Nehemiah's Plan 17

9. Achievements I Desire for This Year 19

10. Value and Mission Statements 22

11. Staying on Track 23

12. Plans for Each Month 25

13. Plans for Each Week—Reflection and Analysis 34

14. Celebrating Successes—Goals I Have Accomplished 60

15. Journaling Your Journey 64

1. RECORD YOUR DREAMS

Journal Your Journey.

This journal is designed for people who need to give life to their dreams! To help you, this journal offers guidance in setting goals and managing the progress needed to achieve your dream. The prophet Nehemiah is the example of the organization; you will see how his plan got results. He used great management skills to get the job done, and so can you!

This book will give you the motivation and inspiration to get you started. We will also ask you to look inward and discard anything that might be keeping you emotionally down. Journaling gives you a chance to see what is in your thoughts and to free your mind of clutter and negative anchors. You can then write the vision of your dreams and goals because you can see and measure your progress with this helpful inspirational journal.

Writing is creative and helps get the energy out of the mind to a place where you can better deal with it. Aspirations committed to paper will cause you to work hard to achieve your goals, you will give birth to your thoughts, which take on real life. With guidance, you can reach your dreams and attain your goals. By journaling, you can track your achievements, measure progress, plan your actions, yearly, monthly, weekly and daily. This book is the support you need to face life's challenges, you are now on the road to success.

This journal also allows you to use time management to stay focused as you make real progress.

- You will start by identifying what you can make happen in **one year**.
- Look at **each month** of the year and determine how you can work in that month to get closer to your goals for one year.
- Next, within each month, you will assign for **each week** the right actions to meet the goals for that week so that you can complete the month's endeavors successfully.
- At the end of the month, **evaluate your goals and your actions**. Then record in your journal what went right and what needs improvement.
- The "**Reflect and analyze**" sheets will give you space to look at your plans and goals to see if they are realistic and attainable.
- **Daily** use the calendar on your cell phone to remind yourself of the action for the day.
- This journal encourages you to **commit to following** your plans.

Goal setting + organization + commitment (be determined to carry out your plans) = success. You must follow your plans!

Give your dreams a chance! Move your life forward. Don't be afraid to set out on a journey of faith in God and faith in yourself. You can go farther, and we are encouraging you to try.

Journal your dreams until they take wings.

Find Your Wings

Write down your dreams.

Feel free to write anything (avoid details).

1. _____
2. _____
3. _____
4. _____
5. _____
6. _____
7. _____

Believe in something larger than yourself. (Barbara Bush)

If thou canst believe, all things are possible to him that believeth. (Mark 9:23)

In all thy ways acknowledge him, and he shall direct thy path. (Proverbs 3:6)

Isaiah 41:10 Fear thou not; for I am with thee: be not dismayed; for I am thy God: I will strengthen thee; yea, I will help thee; yea, I will uphold thee with the right hand of my righteousness.

Journal your journey.
Write your thoughts and topics of interest about journaling.

_____
_____
_____
_____
_____
_____
_____
_____
_____
_____
_____
_____
_____
_____
_____
_____
_____
_____
_____
_____
_____
_____
_____
_____
_____
_____
_____
_____
_____
_____
_____

2. FIRST THINGS FIRST!

We must honor God first. Then we must accomplish the deeds that reflect His will. He will give us a "God idea," and then we must have the faith to pursue that idea. We must next make a step of faith: Believe and trust that God will guide you to do His will. We must then be watchful for His guidance. We must prepare ourselves to be ready when the doors open. Most importantly, we must plan to plan, and reach out to make dreams come true.

What would it take for you to live your dream?

In a list, write down ideas and things you want to pursue.

_____

_____

_____

_____

_____

_____

_____

_____

_____

_____

_____

_____

_____

_____

_____

_____

_____

_____

Once you make up your mind, the fear diminishes. (Rosa Parks)

Nothing so fatiguing as the eternal hanging on of an uncompleted task. (William James)

3. WHAT IS HOLDING YOU BACK?

Fears? Excuses? People? Opinions? Preparation? Faults?

_____

_____

_____

_____

_____

_____

_____

_____

_____

_____

_____

_____

_____

What goals would I like to achieve? Is there anything that I need to improve?

_____

_____

_____

_____

_____

_____

_____

_____

_____

_____

_____

_____

Proverbs 17:8 A gift is as a precious stone in the eyes of him that hath it: withersoever it turneth, it prospereth.

Journal your journey.
Write about your talents and gifts.
Write about your thoughts and topics of interest.

_____
_____
_____
_____
_____
_____
_____
_____
_____
_____
_____
_____
_____
_____
_____
_____
_____
_____
_____
_____
_____
_____
_____
_____

4. BEFORE A NEW YEAR, REMOVE SOME OBSTACLES.

Before I start a new year, I will organize my thoughts!

I need to **remove some emotional anchors** that keep me tied down.

I need to **break free** and untie these anchors.

WHAT COULD THEY BE?

Worry? Worry brings sadness, hurt, depression, idleness, nervousness, anxiety, and unbelief.

Worry is distressing, ruminative fear about events that might occur. In 1 John 4:18, we read about fear: "There is no fear in love; but perfect love casteth out fear: because fear hath torment."

Complaining? People **complain** to gain attention.

They may also **complain** because they are unsatisfied or jealous.

They may be unthankful, faithless, or controlling.

Complaints express dissatisfaction, pain, or distress. In some situations, one can make a formal complaint, accusations or resentment may be involved.

Unbelief? Those suffering from **unbelief** don't realize the truth.

Perhaps they don't really know God.

Perhaps they feel doubts, and keep failures alive, or suffer disappointment.

Perhaps they are faithless.

A person demonstrating **unbelief** may be incredulous or skeptical.

Incredulous can mean *unwilling to admit or accept* what is offered as truth.

Skepticism is the opinion that nothing can be known with certainty.

What **anchors** keep you from living a more victorious life? Could you be constrained by fear, drugs, failures, brokenness, rejections, or abuse? What are your constraints? It's time to break free, cut that anchor loose, stop sitting beside burdens that have a hold upon you, and if they are holding you back, face them and work to break free resolve to correct any obstacles.

Write about what holds you down. What anchors do you need to cut loose?

_____

_____

_____

_____

_____

_____

Decide to move forward. Describe what you should do to move forward.

_____

_____

_____

What changes do you need to make to start a new behavior? Find scriptures that will help direct the changes. Anchor yourself in Jesus. Anchor yourself in the Word of God because His Word is truth.

I need to change;

_____

_____

_____

_____

_____

_____

_____

_____

_____

_____

_____

Galatians 5:22-23 But the fruit of the Spirit is love, joy, peace, longsuffering, gentleness, goodness, faith, meekness, temperance: against such, there is no law.

Journal your journey. List self-improvement and motivational ideas. Record thoughts and issues of interest.

_____

_____

_____

_____

_____

_____

_____

_____

_____

_____

_____

_____

_____

_____

_____

_____

_____

_____

_____

_____

_____

_____

_____

_____

_____

_____

_____

_____

_____

5. LET'S TAKE A GOOD LOOK INSIDE

Do you lack organizational skills?

Are you afraid to set goals because you fear failure?

Are you the world's best procrastinator?

Have you heard negative comments about you?

Do you hear a negative tape that plays in your head? Does the voice say; I can't finish things? Are they right? I'm not very smart.

Does it say; I am a needy person? I need someone to help me. I can't do things by myself. I need somebody else to make me happy.

Does it say, "I am always the last one"?

Do you ask yourself, "Why am I always angry?"

Do "you" have too much mental traffic?

It's that time

It's time to improve yourself. It's time to discard negative assessments and proceed to better thoughts about yourselves. Read books that promote positive thinking. Seek out good motivational seminars. Resist being negative. Each day, say, "I am blessed" at least thirty times in one minute, several times a day.

The Bible is a great book that promotes positive thinking. Remember the message of Romans 12:2: "And be not conformed to this world: but be ye transformed by the renewing of your mind, that ye may prove what is that good and acceptable and perfect will of God." The Bible tells you to renew your mind, look up, and live on higher ground because looking up pulls you up. The psalmist offers the same encouragement in Psalm 121:1—"I will lift up my eyes to the hills from which cometh my help."

2 Corinthians 5:7 For we walk by faith, not by sight

Journal your journey.
How is your faith?
Write thoughts and topics of interest.

_____
_____
_____
_____
_____
_____
_____
_____
_____
_____
_____
_____
_____
_____
_____
_____
_____
_____
_____
_____

6. GOAL SETTING

Goals are set for the following reasons.

1. Goals provide specific directions for your efforts.
2. Goals give meaning to your choices.
3. Goals develop self-control, self-esteem, and self-confidence.
4. Goals put you in charge.
5. Goals get you ready for the opportunity.
6. Goals let you plan where you want to go.
7. Short-term and intermediate goals give you continued successes as you move toward your long-term goals.
8. Goals give you a guide to measure your progress.

Life is a learning journey. Success is a reward of productive planning and the achievement of specific goals.

Know that goals are set with the purpose of improvement. Goal setting will improve your future, and commit to following goals will make you successful.

Life will have its challenges—stumbling blocks and even failures. However, when we set goals and stick to timelines, we won't get stuck or quit along the way. We should all seek to realize achievements, both small and great "is" progress. Stumbling blocks are really stepping stones.

2 Peter 4:4 Ye are of God, little children, and have overcome them: because greater is he that is in you than he that is in the world.

Journal your journey. Face your fears. Write thoughts and topics of interest.

_____
_____
_____
_____
_____
_____
_____
_____
_____
_____
_____
_____
_____
_____
_____
_____
_____
_____
_____
_____
_____
_____
_____
_____
_____
_____
_____
_____
_____

7. NEW MOTIVATION OR INSPIRATION

Year: _____

Date: _____

My journey journal for the New Year

The purpose for life is a life with purpose. (Rick Warren)

O give thanks unto the Lord; for he is good: for his mercy endureth forever. (Psalm 136:1)

If you fail to plan, then you plan to fail.

The six *P*s of success: Prior proper planning prevents poor performance.

The six *P*s of failure: Poor planning precedes poor personal performance.

Write any quotations, scriptures, or mentors that have help to guide you in life:

_____
_____
_____
_____
_____
_____
_____
_____
_____
_____
_____
_____
_____
_____
_____
_____
_____
_____

Galatians 6:9 And let us not be weary in well doing for in due season we shall reap, if we faint not.

Journal your journey. Don't give up! Write some affirmations—positive words or convictions.

1. Yes, I can plan and organize my goals and plans_____

2._____

3._____

4._____

5._____

6._____

7._____

8._____

9._____

10._____

11._____

12._____

13._____

14._____

15._____

16._____

8. NEHEMIAH'S PLAN

In the book of Nehemiah, you will find great examples of management skills, organizational skills, and strategies that are as revealing as any book on the best seller list.

Around 445 BC, Israel was in exile. Jerusalem, the Jews' holy city, had been destroyed. Jerusalem lacked leadership. There was no one to show them where to start or what direction to take to revive the city. Nehemiah heard about the condition of the city, and he wanted to remove the shame of Jerusalem by rebuilding the walls.

A brief summary of Nehemiah's approach to problem-solving and goal setting

1. He heard the problem.
2. Nehemiah first prayed. He continued to pray.
3. He took action. He prioritized his actions: first things first.
4. With permission, he left Persia and went to Jerusalem. He was patient.
5. He took the time to analyze the situation and carefully considered the issues, the dangers, and the people.
6. He then stated the problem, figured out a plan, and checked his information. He made sure his plan would work and was realistic.
7. He presented his plan with confidence to the leaders and people.
8. He organized the work of the people, and he also followed up with several meetings.
9. He solved problems among the people. The rich took advantage of the poor. He used God's laws and commandments to settle disputes.
10. He showed integrity, fairness, kindness, and godliness.
11. He had to confront problems, plots, lies, and enemies. (Don't get into situations that are not godly or not according to God's Word.)
12. He had the priest read God's law to the people, and their hearts were turned back to God. (Always read God's Word.)
13. With cooperation and God's leadership, the wall was finished.
14. Nehemiah established policies for Jerusalem.
15. They celebrated their victory and dedicated the wall with planned praise and thanksgiving.

God wants us to succeed. He will lead us as we pray. Use your mind and prepare yourself. Be ready for the blessings. When preparation meets opportunity there will be increase and promotion.

Romans 12:11 Not slothful in business; fervent in spirit; serving the Lord.

Journal your journey. Don't be lazy. Work hard! Write thoughts and topics of interest.

_____
_____
_____
_____
_____
_____
_____
_____
_____
_____
_____
_____
_____
_____
_____
_____
_____
_____
_____
_____
_____
_____
_____
_____
_____
_____
_____
_____
_____
_____
_____

9. ACHIEVEMENTS I DESIRE FOR THIS YEAR

✞ Ministry or Spirituality

_____
_____
_____
_____

✞ Career

_____
_____
_____
_____

✞ Physical

_____
_____
_____
_____

✞ Educational

_____
_____
_____
_____

✞ Financial

_____
_____
_____
_____

✝ Social

_____

_____

_____

_____

✝ Family

_____

_____

_____

_____

What might prevent you from having real achievements or success (circle one or more)?

- procrastination
- inner conflict
- grief
- habits
- lack of self-control
- priorities
- people
- negativity
- problems
- fears
- anxiety / nervousness
- anger

It may help to look up the definition of the word you circled, look at the adjectives that describe the word. Now make a list of words of opposite actions or qualities. Now that you are aware of the negatives and the positives target the habits that will help you move to be the un-anchored person you want to be. Work to conquer the inner conflict and attitudes that hold you back.

Try doing one of these helpful hints:

1. Find a class to take for self-improvement.
   Online classes / Audio Books
2. Purchase a book that will "up left" you and help you improve.
3. Join an organization that will give you examples of positive behavior.
4. The library now offers a book club that meets and discusses their reading.
5. Use some of the positive principles that you have begun to collect, write them down and start to practice them weekly.
6. What actions have you identified that can be improved? Write down the changes you should make and work at being a better YOU. Why not make "self–improvement" one of your personal goals. What a great time to use this journal to achieve this important goal.

People and your environment may have caused you to face some challenges but you can work to deal with any issue and make a change! Always work to improve your environment and yourselves as well. You are more than able to achieve good results.

10. VALUE AND MISSION STATEMENTS

My value statements

I value _____

I value _____

I value _____

I value _____

My mission statement

_____

_____

_____

_____

_____

_____

_____

What are my gifts and talents? _____

What is my purpose in life as I see it now? _____

11. STAYING ON TRACK

My prayer for guidance for each week:

_____

_____

_____

_____

_____

People I want to pray for:

1. _____
2. _____
3. _____
4. _____
5. _____
6. _____

Situations I want to pray for:

1. _____

2. _____

3. _____

4. _____

My commitment statement:

_____

_____

_____

_____

Proverbs 22:4 By humility and the fear of the Lord are riches, and honor, and life.

Journal your journey. Why am I journaling my dreams? Write thoughts, revisit your purpose.

_____
_____
_____
_____
_____
_____
_____
_____
_____
_____
_____
_____
_____
_____
_____
_____
_____
_____
_____
_____
_____
_____
_____
_____
_____
_____
_____
_____

12. PLANS FOR EACH MONTH

Please fill this section out. The process begins here. It serves as a timeline for your goals. This planner will help you see what must be done to make an "action plan." Evaluate your progress at the end of each month.

January

_____

_____

_____

_____

End-of-month evaluation: _____

_____

February

_____

_____

_____

_____

End-of-month evaluation: _____

_____

March

_____

_____

_____

_____

End-of-month evaluation: _____

_____

✝ Continue to evaluate.   Have faith.

April

_____

_____

_____

_____

_____

End-of-month evaluation: _____

_____

May

_____

_____

_____

_____

_____

End-of-month evaluation: _____

_____

June

_____

_____

_____

_____

_____

End-of-month evaluation: _____

_____

✠ Evaluate the first six months: _____

_____

_____

_____

_____

July

_____

_____

_____

_____

_____

_____

_____

End-of-month evaluation: _____

_____

August

_____

_____

_____

_____

_____

_____

_____

End-of-month evaluation:_____

_____

September

_____

_____

_____

_____

_____

_____

_____

End-of-month evaluation: _____

_____

October

_____

_____

_____

_____

_____

End-of-month evaluation: _____

_____

November

_____

_____

_____

_____

_____

End-of-month evaluation: _____

_____

December

_____

_____

_____

_____

_____

End-of-month evaluation: _____

_____

✠ Evaluate the last six months:_____

_____

_____

_____

_____

Ecclesiastes 3:13 And also that every man should eat and drink, and enjoy the good of all his labor, it is the gift of God

Journal your journey.
Plan well. Get help from_____ (book / mentor)
Write thoughts and topics of interest.

_____
_____
_____
_____
_____
_____
_____
_____
_____
_____
_____
_____
_____
_____
_____
_____
_____
_____
_____
_____
_____
_____
_____
_____
_____
_____
_____
_____

13. PLANS FOR EACH WEEK—REFLECTION AND ANALYSIS

Use the plans identified from the MONTH to target each WEEK's project to do! These "To-Do" actions will guide your steps to accomplish one needed action. You are moving closer!

Each week you are making progress to reach January's goal, as you manage your time wisely!

Next! Put the needed actions for the DAY, as events, on your cell phone calendar (a reminder)!

January

First week, dates: _____

_____

_____

_____

_____

Second week, dates: _____

_____

_____

_____

_____

Third week, dates: _____

_____

_____

_____

_____

Fourth week, dates: _____

_____

_____

_____

_____

Goal setting + organization + commitment (obey your plans) = success.

Ecclesiastes 3:13 And also that every man should eat and drink, and enjoy the good of all his labor, it is the gift of God

Journal your journey.
Plan well. Get help from_____ (book / mentor)
Write thoughts and topics of interest.

_____

_____

_____

_____

_____

_____

_____

_____

_____

_____

_____

_____

_____

_____

_____

_____

_____

_____

_____

_____

_____

_____

_____

_____

_____

_____

_____

_____

_____

_____

13. PLANS FOR EACH WEEK—REFLECTION AND ANALYSIS

Use the plans identified from the MONTH to target each WEEK's project to do! These "To-Do" actions will guide your steps to accomplish one needed action. You are moving closer!

Each week you are making progress to reach January's goal, as you manage your time wisely!

Next! Put the needed actions for the DAY, as events, on your cell phone calendar (a reminder)!

January

First week, dates: _____

_____

_____

_____

_____

Second week, dates: _____

_____

_____

_____

_____

Third week, dates: _____

_____

_____

_____

_____

Fourth week, dates: _____

_____

_____

_____

_____

Goal setting + organization + commitment (obey your plans) = success.

Reflect and analyze

How well did you follow your weekly plans?
Express successes and failures.

January

_____

_____

_____

_____

_____

_____

_____

_____

_____

_____

_____

_____

_____

_____

_____

_____

_____

_____

_____

_____

_____

_____

_____

_____

_____

_____

Remember! Check your plans often and commit to following your plans.

Set plans for each week in the month of_____, the year _____.

Use the plans identified from the MONTH to target each WEEK's project to do! These "To-Do" actions will guide your steps to accomplish one needed action. You are moving closer!

Each week you are making progress to reach February's goal, as you manage your time wisely!

Next! Put the needed actions for the DAY, as events, on your cell phone calendar (a reminder)!

February

First week, dates: _____

_____

_____

_____

_____

Second week, dates: _____

_____

_____

_____

_____

_____

Third week, dates: _____

_____

_____

_____

_____

_____

Fourth week, dates: _____

_____

_____

_____

_____

Goal setting + organization + commitment (be determined to carry out your plans) = success.

Reflect and analyze

How well did you follow your weekly plans?
Express successes and failures.

February

_____

_____

_____

_____

_____

_____

_____

_____

_____

_____

_____

_____

_____

_____

_____

_____

_____

_____

_____

_____

_____

_____

_____

_____

_____

_____

Remember! Check your plans often and commit to following your plans.

Set plans for each week in the month of_____, the year _____.

Use the plans identified from the MONTH to target each WEEK's project to do! These "To-Do" actions will guide your steps to accomplish one needed action. You are moving closer!

Each week you are making progress to reach March's goal, as you manage your time wisely!

Next! Put the needed actions for the DAY, as events, on your cell phone calendar (a reminder)!

March

First week, dates: _____

_____
_____
_____
_____

Second week, dates: _____

_____
_____
_____
_____
_____

Third week, dates: _____

_____
_____
_____
_____
_____

Fourth week, dates:

_____
_____
_____
_____
_____

Goal setting + organization + commitment (obey your plans) = success.

Reflect and analyze

How well did you follow your weekly plans?
Express successes and failures.

March

_____

_____

_____

_____

_____

_____

_____

_____

_____

_____

_____

_____

_____

_____

_____

_____

_____

_____

_____

_____

_____

_____

_____

_____

_____

Remember! Check your plans often and commit to following your plans.

Set plans for each week in the month of_____, the year _____.

Use the plans identified from the MONTH to target each WEEK's project to do! These "To-Do" actions will guide your steps to accomplish one needed action. You are moving closer!

Each week you are making progress to reach April's goal, as you manage your time wisely!

Next! Put the needed actions for the DAY, as events, on your cell phone calendar (a reminder!)

April

First week, dates: _____

_____
_____
_____
_____
_____

Second week, dates: _____

_____
_____
_____
_____
_____

Third week, dates: _____

_____
_____
_____
_____
_____

Fourth week, dates: _____

_____
_____
_____
_____
_____

Goal setting + organization + commitment (be determined to carry out your plans) = success.

Reflect and analyze

How well did you follow your weekly plans?
Express successes and failures.

April

_____

_____

_____

_____

_____

_____

_____

_____

_____

_____

_____

_____

_____

_____

_____

_____

_____

_____

_____

_____

_____

_____

_____

_____

Remember! Check your plans often and commit to following your plans.

Set plans for each week in the month of_____, **the year** _____.

Use the plans identified from the MONTH to target each WEEK's project to do! These "To-Do" actions will guide your steps to accomplish one needed action. You are moving closer!

Each week you are making progress to reach May's goal, as you manage your time wisely!

Next! Put the needed actions for the DAY, as events, on your cell phone calendar (a reminder!)

May

First week, dates: _____

_____
_____
_____
_____
_____

Second week, dates: _____

_____
_____
_____
_____
_____

Third week, dates: _____

_____
_____
_____
_____
_____

Fourth week, dates: _____

_____
_____
_____
_____
_____

Goal setting + organization + commitment (determination to carry out your plans) = success.

Reflect and analyze

How well did you follow your weekly plans?
Express successes and failures.

April

_____
_____
_____
_____
_____
_____
_____
_____
_____
_____
_____
_____
_____
_____
_____
_____
_____
_____
_____
_____
_____
_____
_____
_____
_____

Remember! Check your plans often and commit to following your plans.

Set plans for each week in the month of_____**, the year**_____.

Use the plans identified from the MONTH to target each WEEK's project to do! These "To-Do" actions will guide your steps to accomplish one needed action. You are moving closer!

Each week you are making progress to reach May's goal, as you manage your time wisely!

Next! Put the needed actions for the DAY, as events, on your cell phone calendar (a reminder!)

May

First week, dates: _____

_____
_____
_____
_____
_____

Second week, dates: _____

_____
_____
_____
_____
_____

Third week, dates: _____

_____
_____
_____
_____
_____

Fourth week, dates: _____

_____
_____
_____
_____
_____

Goal setting + organization + commitment (determination to carry out your plans) = success.

Reflect and analyze

How well did you follow your weekly plans?
Express successes and failures.

May

_____
_____
_____
_____
_____
_____
_____
_____
_____
_____
_____
_____
_____
_____
_____
_____
_____
_____
_____
_____
_____
_____
_____
_____
_____
_____
_____

Remember! Check your plans often and commit to following your plans.

Set plans for each week in the month of_____, the year _____.

Use the plans identified from the MONTH to target each WEEK's project to do! These "To-Do" actions will guide your steps to accomplish one needed action. You are moving closer!

Each week you are making progress to reach June's goal, as you manage your time wisely!

Next! Put the needed actions for the DAY, as events, on your cell phone calendar (a reminder)!

June

First week, dates: _____

_____
_____
_____
_____
_____

Second week, dates: _____

_____
_____
_____
_____
_____

Third week, dates: _____

_____
_____
_____
_____
_____

Fourth week, dates: _____

_____
_____
_____
_____
_____

Goal setting + organization + commitment (obey your plans) = success.

Reflect and analyze

How well did you follow your weekly plans?
Express successes and failures.

June

_____

_____

_____

_____

_____

_____

_____

_____

_____

_____

_____

_____

_____

_____

_____

_____

_____

_____

_____

_____

_____

_____

_____

_____

_____

_____

_____

Remember! Check your plans often and commit to following your plans.

Set plans for each week in the month of_____, the year _____.

Use the plans identified from the MONTH to target each WEEK's project to do! These "To-Do" actions will guide your steps to accomplish one needed action. You are moving closer!

Each week you are making progress to reach July's goal, as you manage your time wisely!

Next! Put the needed actions for the DAY, as events, on your cell phone calendar (a reminder)!

July

First week, dates: _____

_____
_____
_____
_____
_____

Second week, dates: _____

_____
_____
_____
_____
_____

Third week, dates: _____

_____
_____
_____
_____
_____

Fourth week, dates: _____

_____
_____
_____
_____
_____

Goal setting + organization + commitment (your efforts will make your plans work) = success.

Reflect and analyze

How well did you follow your weekly plans?
Express successes and failures.

July

_____
_____
_____
_____
_____
_____
_____
_____
_____
_____
_____
_____
_____
_____
_____
_____
_____
_____
_____
_____
_____
_____
_____
_____
_____
_____
_____
_____

Remember! Check your plans often and commit to following your plans.

Set plans for each week in the month of_____**, the year** _____.

Use the plans identified from the MONTH to target each WEEK's project to do! These "To-Do" actions will guide your steps to accomplish one needed action. You are moving closer!

Each week you are making progress to reach August's goal as you manage your time wisely!

Next! Put the needed actions for the DAY, as events, on your cell phone calendar (a reminder)!

August

First week, dates: _____

_____

_____

_____

_____

_____

Second week, dates: _____

_____

_____

_____

_____

_____

Third week, dates: _____

_____

_____

_____

_____

_____

Fourth week, dates: _____

_____

_____

_____

_____

_____

Goal setting + organization + commitment (be determined to carry out your plans) = success.

Reflect and analyze

How well did you follow your weekly plans?
Express successes and failures.

August

_____
_____
_____
_____
_____
_____
_____
_____
_____
_____
_____
_____
_____
_____
_____
_____
_____
_____
_____
_____
_____
_____
_____
_____
_____

Remember! Check your plans often and commit to following your plans.

Set plans for each week in the month of_____, the year _____.

Use the plans identified from the MONTH to target each WEEK's project to do! These "To-Do" actions will guide your steps to accomplish one needed action. You are moving closer!

Each week you are making progress to reach September's goal, as you manage your time wisely!

Next! Put the needed actions for the DAY, as events, on your cell phone calendar (a reminder)!

September

First week, dates: _____

_____

_____

_____

_____

_____

Second week, dates: _____

_____

_____

_____

_____

_____

Third week, dates: _____

_____

_____

_____

_____

_____

Fourth week, dates: _____

_____

_____

_____

_____

_____

Goal setting + organization + commitment (be excited, be wise, be steady) = success.

Reflect and analyze

How well did you follow your weekly plans?
Express successes and failures.

September

_____
_____
_____
_____
_____
_____
_____
_____
_____
_____
_____
_____
_____
_____
_____
_____
_____
_____
_____
_____
_____
_____
_____
_____
_____

Remember! Check your plans often and commit to following your plans.

Set plans for each week in the month of_____, the year _____.

Use the plans identified from the MONTH to target each WEEK's project to do! These "To-Do" actions will guide your steps to accomplish one needed action. You are moving closer!

Each week you are making progress to reach October's goal, as you manage your time wisely!

Next! Put the needed actions for the DAY, as events, on your cell phone calendar (a reminder)!

October

First week, dates: _____

_____
_____
_____
_____
_____

Second week, dates: _____

_____
_____
_____
_____
_____

Third week, dates: _____

_____
_____
_____
_____
_____

Fourth week, dates: _____

_____
_____
_____
_____
_____

Goal setting + organization + commitment (can you see the finish line?) = success.

Reflect and analyze

How well did you follow your weekly plans?
Express successes and failures.

October

_____
_____
_____
_____
_____
_____
_____
_____
_____
_____
_____
_____
_____
_____
_____
_____
_____
_____
_____
_____
_____
_____
_____
_____
_____
_____
_____
_____
_____
_____

Remember! Check your plans often and commit to following your plans.

Set plans for each week in the month of_____, the year _____.

Use the plans identified from the MONTH to target each WEEK's project to do! These "To-Do" actions will guide your steps to accomplish one needed action. You are moving closer!

Each week you are making progress to reach November's goal, as you manage your time wisely!

Next! Put the needed actions for the DAY, as events, on your cell phone calendar (a reminder)!

November

First week, dates: _____

_____

_____

_____

_____

_____

Second week, dates: _____

_____

_____

_____

_____

_____

Third week, dates: _____

_____

_____

_____

_____

_____

Fourth week, dates: _____

_____

_____

_____

_____

_____

Goal setting + organization + commitment (keep obeying your plans) = success.

Reflect and analyze

How well did you follow your weekly plans?
Express successes and failures.

November

_____
_____
_____
_____
_____
_____
_____
_____
_____
_____
_____
_____
_____
_____
_____
_____
_____
_____
_____
_____
_____
_____
_____
_____
_____
_____
_____
_____
_____
_____
_____

Remember! Check your plans often and commit to following your plans.

Set plans for each week in the month of_____**, the year** _____.

Use the plans identified from the MONTH to target each WEEK's project to do! These "To-Do" actions will guide your steps to accomplish one needed action. You are moving closer!

Each week you are making progress to reach December's goal as you manage your time wisely!

Next! Put the needed actions for the DAY, as events, on your cell phone calendar. (a reminder)!

December

First week, dates: _____

_____

_____

_____

_____

_____

Second week, dates: _____

_____

_____

_____

_____

_____

Third week, dates: _____

_____

_____

_____

_____

_____

Fourth week, dates: _____

_____

_____

_____

_____

_____

Goal setting + organization + commitment (you have planned, you are an achiever) = success.

Reflect and analyze

How well did you follow your weekly plans?
Express successes and failures.

December

_____
_____
_____
_____
_____
_____
_____
_____
_____
_____
_____
_____
_____
_____
_____
_____
_____
_____
_____
_____
_____
_____
_____
_____
_____

Remember! Check your plans often and commit to following your plans.

John 20:21 Then said Jesus to them again, Peace be unto you: as my Father hath sent me, so send I you,

Journal your journey through the last month of the year. Write thoughts and topics of interest.

_____
_____
_____
_____
_____
_____
_____
_____
_____
_____
_____
_____
_____
_____
_____
_____
_____
_____
_____
_____
_____
_____
_____
_____
_____
_____
_____
_____
_____
_____
_____
_____

Psalm 119:66 Teach me good judgment and knowledge; for I have believed thy commandments

Journal your journey. Write truthfully about yourself and what you have achieved.

_____

_____

_____

_____

_____

_____

_____

_____

_____

_____

_____

_____

_____

_____

_____

_____

_____

_____

_____

_____

_____

_____

_____

_____

_____

_____

_____

_____

_____

_____

_____

_____

_____

_____

_____

14. CELEBRATING SUCCESSES—GOALS I HAVE ACCOMPLISHED

Goals accomplished

1. _____

2. _____

3. _____

4. _____

5. _____

6. _____

7. _____

8. _____

9. _____

10. _____

11. _____

12. _____

_____

13. _____

_____

14. _____

_____

15. _____

_____

16. _____

_____

17. _____

_____

18. _____

_____

19. _____

_____

_____

Whatsoever things are; true, noble, right, pure, lovely, admirable - if anything is excellent or praiseworthy, think about such things.
(Philippians 4:8, New International Version)

What are your thoughts on things that were important to you? What was your #1 motivation?

_____

_____

_____

_____

_____

_____

_____
_____
_____
_____
_____
_____
_____
_____
_____
_____
_____
_____
_____
_____

Happy is the man that findeth wisdom and the man that getteth understanding. For the merchandise of it is better than the merchandise of silver, and the gain thereof than fine gold. (Proverbs 3:13)

What are your thoughts and observations about your journey?

_____
_____
_____
_____
_____
_____
_____
_____
_____
_____
_____
_____
_____
_____
_____

15. JOURNALING YOUR JOURNEY

Lessons of life

Find your direction! The inner and outer directions for your goals and dreams lie in your discovery of what you want, of where you choose to go, and in researching how to get there. Life is a journey that can be left to chance—or you can direct your life in the way that gives your life meaning and purpose. Learn as much as you can about what you want to achieve. Try to expand your environment. Learn about people, finances, and time management. Read books that encourage positive thinking. Get wisdom from experts, read biographies and autobiographies, grow, and improve your character.

Try joining organizations and groups to get to know people and how they communicate. Be a good listener and an observer of people. Watching them will teach you a lot about character. Don't interrupt others when they are talking because it says to them, "What I have to say is more important than what you have to say." Use good manners when you communicate. Never throw a temper tantrum on paper or in a text message.

Be able to compliment and honor others. Be a positive person and keep the word *hate* out of your vocabulary. Expressing hatred will affect your attitude. For an achiever, a positive attitude is very important. Being positive is an asset and will help keep you motivated and active.

If people compliment you on your abilities, pay attention. They might be pointing out a gift or talent of which you have been unaware. Play to your strengths and invest in your strengths. Perhaps a hobby that you love can become a career.

Spiritual gifts are needed for the body of Christ. Develop a strong spiritual life, always read the Bible and books about the people in the Bible, go to conferences, and learn from other gifted people. Be a giver: Give the Lord prayers, songs, praise, and your time, talent, and treasure. The Lord is a rewarder, and he will give you blessings for submitting your life to him.

Love others and seek, to be honest, and forgiving. Your life depends on how well you love and forgive. Always develop your abilities; never think that you have all that it takes. When the rug gets pulled out from under you, others will be glad to see you fall if they think you had too much pride or ego. Be willing to learn! Anyone can teach you something new if you are willing to learn.

Goals keep you striving to achieve something greater or better. You help the world move around because you are moving. Use your energy and strength. Be determined and don't stop striving to improve yourself. Work the seven *up*s: Look up, get up, raise up, move up, speak up, show up, and never give up.

It is said that some Native Americans tribes do not have a word for *work* because life is work. Work hard! Your life is worth the work! Life is a battle, so prepare to fight your battles. Preparation is the key to success. Remember that when preparation meets opportunity, it produces blessings and promotion. However, if something strange happens, no one can take away what you have learned or experienced, and with the wisdom, you have developed, you will still win. Perhaps you just need to take a different action.

As you journal your journey, I pray that you will be blessed to achieve your dreams.

BIBLIOGRAPHY

New Webster's Dictionary and Thesaurus. Danbury, CT, Lexicon Publications, Inc., 1993.

Zodhiates, Spiros. *The Hebrew-Greek Key Word Study Bible,* KJV Edition. Chattanooga, TN: AMG Publishers, 1991.

Life Application Study Bible, NIV. Edited by Ronald A. Beers. Wheaton, IL: Tyndale House Publishers, Inc., 1997.

Printed in the United States
By Bookmasters